# THE X/TWITTER MONEY BIBLE

How to Make Money on X and Make the Algorithm
Work for You

## IBRAHIM JOHN

**Nzunda Technologies Limited**

# TABLE OF CONTENTS

# INTRODUCTION

I have written this book in such a way that it will remain evergreen. That is, no matter what changes may occur on X, the principles will remain the same.

Also, I have organized it in a way that eliminates the need for memorization; simply read through it, and you will thank me later.

To enhance understanding, I have included illustrations and infographics to simplify complex concepts.

This book is intended for all X creators and those who aspire to make a living on X while maximizing their revenue potential on X/Twitter.

The book is written in a manner that allows the strategies and knowledge it contains to be applied to other two social media platforms namely Facebook and Thread.

The aim is to help creators never leave money on the table and to fully seize all opportunities on X.

You see, when Elon Musk took over Twitter and rebranded it as X, he envisioned it as "the everything app."

He not only opened up its algorithm to the world but also ushered in a new ways to make money on X.

Therefore, through this book, titled "The X/Twitter Money Bible," we embark on a quest to decode and exploit its features and algorithms, unveiling strategies to turn your digital presence into a lucrative venture.

Our expedition is structured into layers for better understanding:

We will start with strategies for establishing a reputable profile. We will examine all the factors and measurements used, as well as strategies to achieve them.

We will delve into the core metrics that the X algorithm utilizes to gauge user reputation and interaction quality.

We will explore how X algorithms work within their background niches/groups, the factors they consider, and strategies to make X work in our favor.

We have revealed visibility Retention Tactics – tactics to ensure your content remains visible by examining the parameters used by the X Algorithm. This will increase the chances of engagement and revenue generation.

You will get acquainted with X recommendation and Viral Triggers. You will know the strategies and signals that can propel your content into viral status, thereby expanding your reach exponentially.

Also, we have laid out strategies on How to Maximize Your X Revenues and Utilize the Platform to Its Full Potential - We will also look into the implications of various elements, such as Post Value Indicators, Recency Effect, Media Files Effect, and Long-Form Content Effect.

These will be scrutinized to provide a simplified understanding of the factors that influence the algorithm's behavior toward your content.

Considering Elon Musk's visionary integrations, such as enabling direct payments and transforming X profiles into online storefronts, we will explore how these features can be utilized to create a thriving online business.

We will also examine several "thou shalt not" practices to avoid, ensuring a smooth journey as you venture into monetizing your X profile.

and on our last chapter we will delve into lucrative business models and strategies designed to optimize your earning potential on X.

"The X Money Bible" is more than just a book; with real-world examples, actionable insights, and step-by-step strategies.

This book is geared towards equipping you with the knowledge and tools necessary to turn your X profile into a revenue-generating asset.

Let us begin by exploring your account/profile factors and strategies.

# PROFILE CREDIBILITY STRATEGY: MAKING THE X ALGORITHM SERVE YOU AS AN INFLUENCER

A reputable profile not only garners trust but also significantly influences how the X algorithm perceives and prioritizes your posts, as well as the visibility of your replies, etc.

Here, we'll look into strategies that can increase your profile's credibility.

The X Algorithm uses several factors to determine if you're reputable, influential, and have authority in what you post or comment.

It assigns a measurement from 0 to 100, called "User Mass", to represent your authority or influence on X.

## User Mass Measurements

Mass represents a user's influence or reputation on X, calculated using various factors.

The code from `UserMass.scala` reveals that the factors utilized include the following:

- Account Age
- Number of Followers and Followings
- Device Usage
- Safety Status (Restricted, Suspended, Verified)

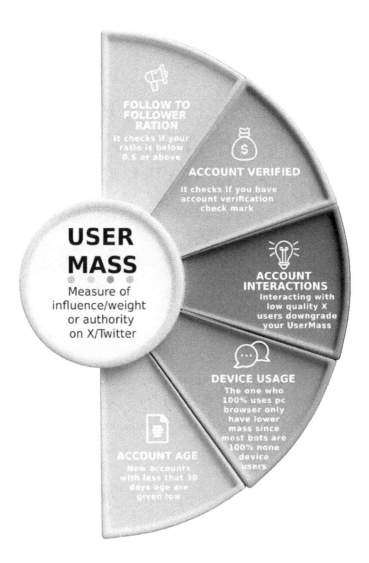

**Strategies to increase your "User Mass:**

Make sure your account is not less than 30 days old.

Use your phone regularly to post, in addition to PC browsers.

Because Bots tend to use web browsers only, so X considers this as a factor. You can use PC browsers, but also use messaging devices occasionally to tell the system that your not a bot.

Avoid actions that may lead to being Restricted or Suspended.

### Other factors used to adjust your account Mass (weight of influence/authority) include the following:

1. Following/Follower Ratio:

This ratio reflects a user's genuineness and influence. A more favorable ratio is seen as indicative of a genuine or influential account, as illustrated in the `Reputation.scala` and `UserMass.scala` files of the X algorithm.

Factors Utilized:

- Number of Followings
- Number of Followers

A formula $(1.0 + numFollowings) / (1.0 + numFollowers)$ is used by the X algorithm to calculate the follower/following ratio, which impacts a user's reputation score.

Also, they have assigned a threshold ratio which 0.6

See its implications bellow;

### Following/Follower Ratio Implications:

A balanced follower/following ratio indicates authenticity on X. A ratio below 0.6 avoids penalties or downranking.

Downranking is done by applying other formula which I will not mention in this book to remove complexities.

But you have to know that there are downranks if your following to follower ratio is above 0.6

Let's consider two examples. John Doe and Elon Musk are both X premium/verified users.

Elon Musk follows 453 accounts and has approximately 158.6M followers.

John Doe follows 6 accounts and has 18 followers.

Using the formula (1.0 + numFollowings) / (1.0 + numFollowers), both have ratios below 0.6,

so no downgrading occurs. Verified accounts receive a Mass of 100, which is not reduced due to a good following/follower ratio.

### Strategies:

Engage with influential accounts. Because X uses the PageRank algorithm, originally developed by Google, to determine influence.

PageRank represents influence of your account in the network.

Quality Content Sharing: Share content that attracts genuine followers.

Stop popular "Follow-for-Follow" Tactics

Avoid practices that distort your ratio.

Be selective following: Initially, follow credible and influential users within your niche.

**Strategies to get your initial followers (for new accounts)**

- Just do a Cross-Platform Promotion: Encourage friends to follow you on X using other platforms like SMS, WhatsApp, or Telegram.

The aim to be followed by X premium/verified users for increased visibility.

- Also Subscribe to X Premium for verification and access to premium features. Just meet X's verification criteria to enhance credibility and reach.

Have Quality Interactions: Because Interactions, especially with credible and verified users, boost credibility.

**Here are Factors Utilized:**

- Interaction with Verified Users
- Interaction with Credible Accounts
- Frequency of Interaction with Spam or Bot Accounts

Hence engage with Verified Accounts through comments, retweets, or mentions.

Avoid chatting and replaying to Bots and Spam in your interactions.

- Participate in Genuine Discussions.
- Community Building:
- Foster genuine relationships through interaction.

### Additional Tips:

### 1. Consistent Branding:

Maintain a consistent brand across your profile with good profile cover photo.

A professional profile picture and cover photo contribute to the first impression and Craft an engaging profile description.

**2. The Language** decided the broadness of the audience to have. Hence a proper language and grammar are crucial for credibility.

If you want to use English language in your post and you are not fluent the just use translation tools for accuracy if English isn't your first language.

I recommend using ChatGPT for translation, because it can translate your language by using context-based translation and not word to word translation. It has human level translation capabilities.

> 3. Also **Share valuable content related to your niche**. So your can engage with authoritative figures in your niche so that the algo can boost your credibility since it uses page rank system of ranking.

# X VISIBILITY RETENTION STRATEGIES.

X recommends **your profile** in the "Who to Follow" section to new users whom it thinks may follow you, also it shows **your posts** to your followers in their timeline, those who have interacted with you, and to new users whom it believes share the same interests as your posts, even if they don't know you.

The foundation for this is recent data, which ensures an accurate relevance score. Therefore, they have established what they call a "lookback window" on each viewer signal/interaction.

A "lookback window" refers to a specific period of time in the past, starting from the current moment, during which data or events are considered or used by algorithm for analysis or processing.

It's used to specify how far back in time certain events or actions are considered or used for decision making in the algorithm.

For example, if a lookback window for a specific user action (like favoriting your post) is set to 90 days, it means that when analyzing or processing data, any user action that occurred within the last 90 days from the current date will be considered.

Any action of favoriting a tweet that took place before this 90-days window will be ignored.

Therefore, if I publish another post within 90 days of my last post, it's more likely that the X algorithm will display my post to the user who liked my previous post.

However, if was quite for more than 90 days, then afterward I post, it's more likely that X will not show my new post to that same viewer/user, meaning I will have lost that user from my sphere of reach.

These lookback windows are crucial for algorithms and for your visibility retention. They help in:

1. Limiting Data Volume By considering only recent data, systems can operate more efficiently without being overwhelmed by the entirety of historical data.

2. Relevance Older data might not be as relevant to current trends or behaviors. By focusing on a specific lookback window, analyses can be more aligned with recent patterns.

In the context of X's recommendation algorithm, a lookback window ensures that the algorithm gives importance to recent user interactions, making the recommendations more relevant to the user's current interests and behaviors.

Here's a list of signals from the provided code along with their respective lookback windows:

### 1. Tweet-based signals

| Signal Name | Lookback window (days) |
|---|---|
| Post Share | 14 |
| Tweet Favorite | 90 |
| Retweet | 90 |
| Reply | 90 |
| Video View | 90 |

NB: these are few signals but there are hundreds/thousands used by algorithm.

### 2. User-based signals

| Signal Name | Lookback |
|---|---|

| | window (Days) |
|---|---|
| AccountFollow | Infinite |
| RepeatedProfileVisit_14D_MinVisit2_V1 | 14 |
| RepeatedProfileVisit_90D_MinVisit6_V1 | 90 |
| RepeatedProfileVisit_180D_MinVisit6_V1 | 180 |
| TrafficAttributionProfile_30D_LastVisit | 30 |
| TrafficAttributionProfile_30D_DecayedVisit | 30 |

## 3. Notifications-based signals

- `NotificationOpenAndClick_V1`: 90 days (with negative events being filtered)

## 4. Negative signals:

| Signal Name | Lookback Windows (days) |
|---|---|
| AccountBlock | Not specified |
| AccountMute | Not specified |
| TweetDontLike | 90 days |
| TweetSeeFewer | 90 days |
| TweetReport | 90 days |

## Key Implications:

Posting less often results in less data for X's algorithm to utilize, diminishing the reach of your posts.

The algorithm tends to "forget" inactive profiles, causing a notable drop in impressions.

More frequent posting supplies fresh data to the algorithm, enhancing the visibility of your posts and profile while increasing the probability of other users discovering your posts and profile.

If users interact with your posts within the lookback windows, they're more likely to see your future posts.

Regular, high-quality posting enlarges the data pool linked to your profile account, expands your reach, elevates your ranking in X's algorithm, and augments your overall visibility and impressions.

See what this X user said.

More 𝕏 algorithm observations:

* Don't miss a day! My impressions dropped from 44.5M (in May) to 13.5M (in July) because I took a week off social media. I knew it would happen but by the time I grew enough for me and every year I take a week off from social media to re-charge. But if you're growing your account, post every day, better few times a day (your content that contributes to the conversation)

Consistency is Key: maintaining a daily presence on X amplifies your reach, audience engagement, ranking, visibility, and impressions on both your profile and posts.

Your followers have an infinite lookback window, meaning they can act as a benchmark.

X examines the latest interests and interactions of your followers to determine if your post might appeal to other non-followers with similar interests.

It also starts with your followers to see how they react to your post and expands its visibility to other audiences. So don't be shy to ask people to follow you if they find what you post is valuable to them.

These parameters highlight the importance of both long-term and short-term engagements with users.

For instance, an infinite lookback on follows suggests a lasting impact, while shorter windows on profile visits indicate a need for continuous engagement.

**Strategy Based on the above Algorithm Insights**

1. Consistent and Regular Posting:

Maintain a steady presence to provide fresh data to X's algorithm.

Develop a content calendar to ensure regular posting, aiming for at least one post per day.

2. Engage Your Followers Actively:

Leverage the infinite lookback window of followers to enhance post visibility.

Create content that encourages interaction (likes, retweets, comments) from followers and ask them to follow you if they find your content valuable.

3. Quality Over Quantity:

Ensure that each post is of high quality to maximize engagement.

Focus on creating content that is relevant, valuable, and interesting to your followers and potential new followers.

Keep an eye on engagement per post and unfollow rates to ensure content quality is maintained.

4. Leverage Short-Term Engagement Windows:

Utilize shorter lookback windows effectively to keep your profile in the algorithm's favorable view.

Implement strategies like polls, Q&A sessions, and trending topic discussions to encourage short-term engagements like profile visits.

Track profile visits, participation in polls/Q&A, and engagement with trending topic posts.

## 5. Encourage and Acknowledge Interactions:

Ensure users who interact with your posts continue to see your future content.

Engage with users who interact with your posts through likes, comments, and retweets. Consider shout-outs or thank-you posts for active followers.

Monitor retention of engaging followers and interaction levels on subsequent posts.

## 6. Diversify Content Types:

Cater to varied interests and interactions of followers and potential audience.

Mix up your content types – images, videos, text, and links – to appeal to a wider audience and explore what gains the most traction.

Analyze which content types are gaining the most engagement and adjust your strategy accordingly.

## 9. Collaborate and Participate:

Expand your reach and visibility through collaborations and participation in wider X activities.

Engage in collaborations with other profiles, participate in trending hashtags, and join X chats or threads relevant to your niche.

Implementing this strategy will require regular reviews and potential adjustments to align with the ever-evolving nature of social media algorithms and audience preferences.

Always keep the user at the center of your strategy, ensuring that while you aim to please the algorithm, your content remains authentic, valuable, and engaging to your audience.

# THE RECENCY EFFECT: THE ADVANTAGES OF NEW POSTS

A new/recent post has a significant advantage over old posts due to the way X's ranking algorithm operates, particularly through parameters like halflife and relevance time.

These parameters help the platform determine how posts are displayed on users' feeds and in search results, emphasizing the freshness and relevance of the content.

It has two parameters which are half-life and Relevance Time, as explained below:

### Your Post/Tweet Half-life:

The half-life parameter is a measure of the time it takes for a post's relevance score to reduce by half compared to a new post.

For instance, if the half-life is set at 6 hours, a post that is 6 hours old would have its relevance score halved, and this process continues as the post ages. The shorter the half-life, the quicker a post loses its relevance score over time, giving a significant advantage to newer posts.

### Relevance Time:

The relevance time refers to the duration a post remains relevant on the platform.

With X's recent update, this duration has been extended **to 48 hours**, meaning posts can stay relevant and appear on feeds for up to 48 hours.

But despite this extension, newer posts still hold an advantage as they start with a higher relevance score which degrades over time based on the half-life parameter.

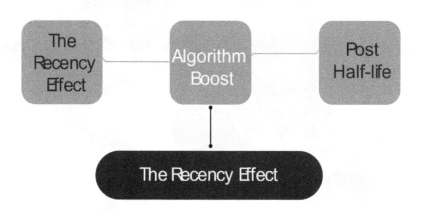

So, the interplay between the half-life and the relevance time creates a scenario where new posts are more likely to be seen and engaged with by users due to their higher initial relevance score.

This score diminishes over time as dictated by the half-life, making the window of optimal engagement narrower for older posts, especially as they move beyond the half-life threshold.

Also, the extension of relevance time to 48 hours does allow for quality content to remain visible for a longer period, but it doesn't negate the advantage held by newer posts.

New posts, having a full relevance score, are more likely to be pushed to the top of users' feeds or search results, thereby garnering more visibility and engagement.

**Here are some strategies to leverage these algorithmic parameters for better post visibility and engagement:**

- **Quality Over Quantity:** Focus on creating high-quality, engaging content. Quality posts are more likely to retain a higher relevance score over the extended halflife, thus staying visible and engaging to the audience for a longer period.
- **Algorithm-Friendly Content:** Utilize formats favored by the X algorithm, like long-form posts and videos, to enhance the chances of your content maintaining a high relevance score.

### Here is what Elon Musk said;

**Elon Musk** ✔ ✖ 👤 @elonmusk · Oct 3

Replying to @MarioNawfal

Interesting.

Our algorithm tries to optimize time spent on X, so links don't get as much attention, because there is less time spent if people click away.

Best thing is to **post** content in **long form** on this platform.

💬 320        🔁 527        ♡ 2,483        ᯤ 268.5K        ⬆

- **Schedule your posts strategically** to ensure maximum visibility and engagement. Knowing that your content has a longer shelf-life allows for better planning and timing of your posts.
- **Engagement:** Prompt engagement by asking questions or sparking discussions in your posts. Engagements can rejuvenate the relevance score of your posts, keeping them visible for longer.

# USER SIGNALS EFFECT: VISIBILITY TRIGGERS

The decision of the X algorithm largely depends on signals or actions taken by viewers as well as the author of the post.

The following are the crucial initial user signals that serve as input for ranking, post visibility, and impressions.

The X algorithm utilizes a mix of both positive and negative user signals to rank and ascertain the visibility of a post.

These signals capture the actions of both the viewers and the post's author.

The weight assigned to each signal profoundly influences the final outcome.

**Positive User Signals**:

| Action | Description |
|---|---|
| Repost | Sharing the post again on one's timeline. |
| Quote | Adding comments while resharing the post. |
| Share | Distributing the post externally or to others. |
| Like/Favorite | Expressing appreciation for the post. |
| Bookmark | Saving the post for later viewing. |
| Media/Photo Expand | Magnifying media or photos included in the post. |
| Dwell Time in Post | Duration spent reading or viewing the post. |
| Dwell Time in Video | Time dedicated to watching a video within the post. |
| Replay | Watching a video in the post multiple times. |
| Author Replay | The post's creator interacting with their own post. |
| Video Play | Initiating a video embedded in the post. |

| Action | Description |
|---|---|
| Spaces | Participating in audio discussions or rooms. |
| Detail Expanded | Delving deeper into the post for more details/reading. |
| User Profile View | Exploring the profile of the post's author. |
| Follow | Subscribing to the post's creator for additional content. |

These actions amplify the post's visibility and have a positive effect on its ranking:

## Negative User Signals:

These actions curtail the post's visibility and might dent its ranking:

| Action | Description |
|---|---|
| Block | Restricting specific content or users. |
| Mute | Suppressing notifications or posts from particular users. |
| Report | Flagging content or behavior as inappropriate. |
| Don't Like | Expressing a lack of interest in certain content. |
| See Fewer | Opting to view less of similar content in the future. |

## What you should do?

Strive to produce content that spurs positive interactions among users.

For instance, the X algorithm suggests that posts accompanied by media often engage users for more extended periods, resulting in heightened interaction.

Such posts also tend to pull in more views or readers on the platform.

Avoid actions or content types that could accrue negative signals.

Engaging in such behaviors could undermine the reach of your content and tarnish the reputation of your profile.

# POST VALUE INDICATORS: HOW TO MAKE X PUSH YOUR POST

There several steps user signals is used to boost your post and increase post visibility.

### Interplay in the Algorithm

The algorithm first assesses the weight of each user interaction.

Then, based on various strategic decisions, multipliers are applied to enhance specific interactions.

Finally, probability rankings predict potential user behavior, dynamically adjusting the final ranking.

For example, a tweet that receives a 'Like' benefits from its base weight.

This weight is then amplified by the multiplier, and the tweet's overall ranking adjusts based on the predicted likelihood of further user interactions.

This table presents some few different user interaction signals and their respective weights, which X algorithm

### Interaction signals and their respective weights

| Signal | Weight |
|--------|--------|
| Detail Expanded | 0.3 |
|  |  |

| Favorited (Likes) | 1 |
|---|---|
| Open Linked | 0.1 |
| Photo Expanded | 0.03 |
| Profile Clicked | 1 |
| Replied | 9 |
| Retweeted (RTs) | 1 |

These weights signify the relevance or influence of each user interaction on the ranking model.

They are then integrated into the algorithm which, in turn, dictates recommendations for the "For You" feed, search results, and the "Who to Follow" section.

Specific multipliers enhance your content's prominence on the platform.

## WEIGHTS VS. MULTIPLIERS VS. PROBABILITY RANKINGS

**Weights**: These are foundational values assigned to specific user interactions, determining their basic importance in the ranking model.

For instance, a favorited (Like) interaction might have a weight of 1.0, suggesting its baseline significance.

**Multipliers:** These act as amplifiers, boosting the influence of certain actions beyond their original weight.

A multiplier enhances the effect of an interaction, often due to external factors or strategic platform decisions.

For example, a "Like" might get a 30x multiplier, thereby increasing its impact on content visibility.

### Probability Rankings:

This is an advanced layer where the algorithm predicts the likelihood of specific user interactions based on historical data and user behavior patterns.

It's more dynamic and **considers the potential future actions of users.**

## X ALGORITHM
## WEIGHTS VS. MULTIPLIERS VS. PROBABILITY RANKINGS

### Weights

These are foundational values assigned to specific user interactions, determining their basic importance in the ranking model

### Multipliers

These act as amplifiers, boosting the influence of certain actions beyond their original weight. They enhances the .effect of an interaction

### Probability Rankings

This is an advanced layer where the algorithm predicts the likelihood of specific user interactions based on his torical data and user behavior patterns.

### X TIMELINE

**Multiplier Effects to Boost Visibility**

| Factor | Multiplier |
|---|---|
| Likes | 30x |
| RTs (Retweets) | 20x |
|  |  |

| Replies | 1x |
|---|---|
| Trusted Circle Engagement | 3x |
| Inclusion of Media | 2x |
| Content in English | [Benefits from wider reach] |
| Gaining Followers | act as initial audience to push your contents |
| Engaging with Trending Topics | 1.1x |
| X Blue Membership | 2-4x |

**Factors Negatively Impacting Visibility**

| Factor | Multiplier |
|---|---|
| Negative User Feedback | -74x |
| Reported Tweets | -369x |

That is; A Negative User Feedback: Actions like "Show Less Often", blocking, or muting have a detrimental multiplier of -74x.

Reported Tweets: A staggering negative multiplier of -369x.

**Content Characteristics which contribute to Lowering Reach:**

- Tweets containing only URLs
- Posts without words or text (e.g. picture only)
- Content with frequent misspellings, fabricated words, or in an unfamiliar language
- Tweets mentioning only a name
- Overuse of hashtags
- Content flagged as misinformation or blacklisted

**Link Limitations:**

While links categorized as "non-news or non-media" might be marked as spam, high engagement due to content relevance can still propel a tweet's virality, albeit starting with a disadvantage.

# Probability Rankings

The "For You" feed showcases tweets based on the likelihood that a user will engage with them in specific ways.

This is determined by a sophisticated ranking algorithm, known as a heavy-ranker.

It assesses multiple features describing both the tweet and the user viewing it, predicting potential user actions. Here's a glimpse of these probabilities:

| User Action | Sentiment | Weight |
|---|---|---|
| Liking your tweet | Positive | 0.5 |
| Retweeting your tweet | Positive | 1 |
| Clicking into your tweet & staying for >2 min | Positive | 11 |
| Visiting your profile via your tweet & engaging | Positive | 12 |
| Replying to your tweet | Positive | 27 |
| Engaging with a reply to your tweet | Positive | 75 |
| Selecting "show less often", blocking, or muting | Negative | -74 |
| Reporting your tweet | Negative | -369 |

## The following are the implications.

- Engaging with a tweet for over 2 minutes is 22x more valuable than a mere like.
- Visiting a profile via a tweet and subsequently interacting is 24x more influential than a like.
- Direct replies to a tweet carry a weight 54x that of a like.
- If a user responds to a reply on their tweet, the effect multiplies to 150x that of a like.
- A reported tweet has a devastating -738x impact compared to a like.

# STRATEGIES TO INCREASE A POST/TWEET'S VALUE AND VISIBILITY

### 1. Leverage High-Impact Interactions

Enhance Engagement: Prioritize actions like retweets and replies due to their high weight. Encourage these actions through CTA's (Calls to Action) in your posts.

Incentivize Replies: Given the weight of replies (9.0), create content that invites discourse and responses.

### 2. Exploit Multiplier Effects

Maximize Like and RT Boosts: Develop content that is universally relatable and shareable to gain likes and retweets.

Engage with Trusted Circle: Encourage frequent interaction within your network for that 3x boost.

Incorporate Media: Use relevant images/videos to gain a 2x multiplier effect.

### 3. Leverage Content Characteristics

Use High-Quality Language: Ensure your posts are well-written, avoiding misspellings and using clear, concise language.

Avoiding Negative Impacts: Strictly avoid content characteristics that can lower reach or result in negative multipliers.

## 4. Utilize Probability Rankings Wisely

Enhance Positive Interactions: Craft posts to drive actions like prolonged engagement (>2 min), profile visits, and engagement with replies due to their high positive weights.

Minimize Negative Actions: Limit content that may encourage users to block, mute, or report your posts to avoid catastrophic negative impacts.

## 5. Engage with Trending and Viral Content

Capitalize on Trends: Engage with trending topics and utilize the 1.1x multiplier to maximize visibility.

Interactive Endings: End tweets with a question to promote engagement and utilize the multiplier effects of replies.

## 6. Integrate a Variety of User Interactions

Varied Engagement: Combine text, images, videos, and other forms of user interaction to cast a wider net and appeal to diverse user behavior.

## 7. Optimize for Inclusive Audience Reach

Use Universal Language: Since content in English has a wider reach, ensure its usage when applicable.

Diverse Content: Ensure that the content is relatable to a broad audience to increase potential engagement.

## 8. Membership and Exclusive Features

Leverage Platform Features: If applicable, utilize X Blue Membership for 2-4x multipliers.

## 9. Incorporate User-Friendly Links

Useful and Relevant Links: Ensure that links are not only relevant but also from trusted sources to avoid being categorized as spam.

## 10. Transparency and Authenticity

Authentic Content: Preserve trust and avoid misinformation labels by always sharing validated and true information.

Clear Messaging: Ensure your content is straightforward, avoiding any potential for misunderstanding or misinterpretation.

# CONTENT CREATION TIPS TO MAKE [X] PUSH YOUR POST

Considering the interaction weights, multipliers, and probability rankings:

Build content that inherently seeks interaction (likes, retweets, and especially replies).

### Quality Visuals:

Since multimedia content has beneficial multipliers, invest in creating high-quality visual content.

"This is what X says on their analytics page.

X Ads     Help?

## Tweets with photos get noticed

It's true. Tweets with images **drive more engagement** and generate more responses.

Learn how to share a photo

Make it a habit to include an image or video with each post. Nowadays, there are tons of image generation tools available to create visuals that relate to the content of your post.

**Storytelling**: Craft your posts to tell a story, enhancing the chance of prolonged engagement and deeper interaction.

User Inclusivity: Ensure that the content is not just high-quality but also inclusive and relatable to a wide user base.

Maintain a consistent posting schedule to keep the audience engaged and the algorithm familiar with regular activity.

Strategies should remain adaptable. As algorithms evolve, it's crucial to revisit, revise, and innovate strategies to align with updated algorithmic functionalities.

Ensure consistent monitoring, learning from metrics, and engaging with your audience genuinely to foster a community around your content, thereby naturally boosting your post's visibility.

# THE LONG FORM
# CONTENT EFFECT

Long-form posts holds a unique power that can significantly influence your success on X. they can be either text based or video au audio(X spaces)

### Why Long-Form Posts Matter?

Long-form posts provide you with the space to explore topics thoroughly and offer **valuable insights**.

This depth is what sets them apart from shorter, superficial content. The more value you provide, the more likely X's algorithm will favor your content.

**Engagement**: Long-form content encourages engagement. When readers invest time in consuming your content, they are more likely to like, comment, and share.

X's algorithm rewards posts that drive engagement because they keep users on the platform longer.

**Establishing Authority:** In-depth posts showcase your expertise and establish you as an authority in your niche.

When X's algorithm detects your expertise, it's more likely to recommend your content to users interested in that topic.

**Dwell Time**: Dwell time is the amount of time users spend on your content.

Long-form posts inherently increase dwell time because readers take longer to consume them.

A longer dwell time signals to X's algorithm that your content is engaging and valuable.

## The Psychology Behind Long-Form Posts

Long-form posts go beyond being a mere collection of words; they tap into the intricate psychology of human interaction and engagement.

Imagine receiving a long, thoughtful message from a friend or colleague.

Would you respond with a curt "thanks" and move on? Chances are, you wouldn't. Here's why:

### Reciprocity Effect of Long-form post:

When someone invests time and effort into delivering value, the reciprocity effect comes into play.

This is a fundamental aspect of human interaction. You feel compelled to reciprocate the effort by engaging more deeply.

In the context of long-form content, readers are more likely to spend time reading, reflecting, and responding because they genuinely appreciate the effort and value you've provided.

**Acknowledgment and Gratitude**: Longer content signals that the creator has invested time and thought into the message.

In response, readers often take more time to digest and respond to the content as a way of acknowledging the effort.

They want to show that they've received, read, and understood the message, often expressing gratitude in their responses.

**Discussion and Interaction**: Lengthy content often sparks more questions, thoughts, and discussions.

When readers encounter valuable insights or thought-provoking ideas, they are more likely to comment, ask questions, or share their own experiences.

This dynamic engagement is favored by social media algorithms, including X's.

**Elon Musk** ✓ X 🔗 @elonmusk · Oct 3

Replying to @MarioNawfal

Interesting.

Our algorithm tries to optimize time spent on X, so links don't get as much attention, because there is less time spent if people click away.

Best thing is to **post** content in **long form** on this platform.

💬 320          🔁 527          ♡ 2,483          ᕱᎯᎯ 268.5K          ⬆

Incorporating this understanding of human psychology into your long-form content strategy can enhance its effectiveness.

The reciprocity effect ensures that when you provide value through long-form content, your audience is more inclined to reciprocate with meaningful interactions, creating a positive feedback loop that benefits both you and your readers.

### The FOMO Effect from long-form posts

But it doesn't end there. Long-form posts also tap into another powerful psychological phenomenon: the fear of missing out (FOMO).

FOMO is the anxiety that people feel when they believe others are experiencing something exciting or valuable without them. When harnessed effectively, FOMO can be a catalyst for expanding your follower base and boosting engagement on X.

**Exclusive Insights:** Long-form content often provides exclusive insights, in-depth knowledge, or behind-the-scenes glimpses that shorter posts can't offer.

When readers encounter such content, they may fear missing out on valuable information if they don't follow your account. This fear can drive them to hit that **"Follow" button.**

**Regular Value**: If you consistently deliver high-quality long-form content, your audience will anticipate and look forward to your posts.

This anticipation can evolve into FOMO, as followers fear missing the next valuable piece of content you'll share, hence prompting them to follow your account.

Community Engagement: Long-form content often fosters vibrant communities of engaged followers.

As people witness these thriving communities, they may fear missing out on the sense of belonging and intellectual stimulation your profile offers.

By acknowledging and leveraging these psychological factors—reciprocity, engagement, and FOMO—you can enhance the impact of your long-form posts on X's algorithm.

This, in turn, will create a more engaging and rewarding content experience for your audience while also expanding your follower base and influence on the platform.

### Implications within X's Algorithm

Understanding how X's algorithm works is crucial for content creators looking to maximize their reach. Here's how long-form posts fit into the algorithm's framework:

**Visibility:** X's algorithm prioritizes content that keeps users engaged and active on the platform. Longer posts have the potential to captivate readers for extended periods, improving your content's visibility.

X values likes, comments, shares, and saves. Long-form posts often generate more of these interactions due to their informative and immersive nature. **The algorithm recognizes this and promotes content with higher engagement metrics**.

**User Satisfaction**: X's ultimate goal is to keep users satisfied and engaged. Long-form content that educates, entertains, or inspires users contributes to this goal, resulting in the algorithm favoring your posts.

**Quality over Quantity:** X's algorithm doesn't prioritize the quantity of content you produce but rather the quality of engagement it generates.

**A single well-crafted long-form post can have a more significant impact than several shorter ones.**

Maximizing the Impact of Long-Form Posts on X's Algorithm

To harness the power of long-form posts within X's algorithm, consider these strategies:

**Consistency:** Maintain a regular posting schedule for long-form content. Consistency helps build your audience and keeps the algorithm engaged.

**Visual Appeal**: Use eye-catching visuals, such as images, infographics, or videos, to complement your long-form posts. These elements can enhance engagement and attract more views.

**Encourage Engagement**: Ask questions, invite opinions, and prompt discussions within your long-form content. Encouraging reader interaction can boost engagement metrics.

**Stay User-Centric**: Focus on providing value to your audience. Address their pain points, answer their questions, and cater your content to their needs and interests.

# THE POST AUTHOR AMPLIFIER EFFECTS. AUTHOR BASED INTERACTION BOOSTING FACTORS

In previous chapters, we examined how viewers' actions/other X users affect the visibility of your post and account.

However, in this section, we will focus on the creator's actions, you the post author.

Let's explore how your own actions on the post will affect its visibility and how they instruct the algorithm accordingly.

| Author/Creator Factors | Boost Multiplier |
|---|---|
| Multiple Hashtags or Trends | 0.6 |
| Indirect Follow | 4 |
| Tweet Includes Trend | 1.1 |
| Self-Tweet (Tweeting to oneself-threads) | 2 |
| Tweet Includes Image URL | 2 |
| Tweet Includes Video URL | 2 |

The "Author Boost Multiplier" signifies how much each factor triggered by you the Author of the post amplifies the visibility or engagement of your post.

For example. From the above table we see that a tweet that incorporates a trending topic (tweetHasTrendBoost) provides a 1.1x boost, indicating a slight increase in visibility or algorithmic preference compared to a tweet without a trend.

Using these multipliers thoughtfully in your social media strategy can assist in enhancing the visibility and engagement of your tweets.

Let's see their implications below.

### Multiple Hashtags or Trends Boost (0.6x)

That is; a tweet containing several hashtags or mentioning multiple trends may receive a 0.6x boost.

Interestingly, this multiplier is less than 1, which might suggest that overuse of hashtags or trends in one post could potentially decrease visibility of that post.

Hence use only One Hashtag per post, use hashtags judiciously and only when they are directly relevant to the content.

Because while hashtags can enhance discoverability, this boost suggests that excessive use or spamming trends can be counterproductive.

Ensure that the hashtags or trends used are currently active and relevant to your audience to maximize engagement.

### Indirect Follow Boost (4.0x)

This means engaging or interacting with users that you do not directly follow may get a significant 4.0x boost.

This is X mechanism to encourage diverse account interactions and expand network reach on the platform.

Therefore, I advise you to engage with a wider array of content and creators.

Retweet, comment, and like posts from users outside of your direct network to maximize visibility and potentially tap into new audience segments.

### Tweet Includes Trend (1.1x)

This is where the importance of hashtag comes into play. That means, including current trends in your tweet can slightly increase its visibility by 1.1x.

Trends are topics or hashtags that are currently popular on the platform.

So, regularly check what's trending and, if applicable, incorporate those trends into your tweets in a meaningful and relevant way.

Ensure that the integration of trends is natural and adds value to the conversation to avoid appearing opportunistic or spammy.

### Self-Tweet (Tweeting to oneself) Boost (2.0x)

Tweeting to oneself, or threading Posts, may double the visibility of the subsequent tweets with a 2.0x boost.

This encourages the creation of more detailed, threaded content.

So, when a single tweet isn't enough to convey your message, don't shy away from threading tweets.

Not only does it allow you to elaborate on topics in more depth, but it also amplifies visibility according to this boost.

Just make sure the thread is cohesive and each tweet adds value to retain audience interest.

### Tweet Includes Image URL Boost (2.0x)

Tweets containing image URLs (likely meaning images are attached) get a 2.0x boost, highlighting the platform's preference for visual content.

Hence integrate high-quality and relevant images into your posts whenever possible.

Visuals not only enhance engagement by capturing attention but also elevate message retention.

### Tweet Includes Video URL Boost (2.0x)

This is like the image URL boost, including a video URL (or attaching a video) doubles visibility with a 2.0x boost.

Utilize videos to convey your messages where relevant. Videos can offer a richer context and evoke responses.

Ensure your videos are of good quality, have clear audio (if applicable), and consider adding captions to enhance accessibility.

**Other factors which you contribute to your post boost and visibility.**

### check your typos.

Ensure all your tweets are grammatically correct and free from typos.

Employ tools like ChatGPT or Grammarly to refine your text, ensuring clarity and safeguarding against potential algorithmic penalties for using misspelled or unrecognized words.

Accurate, legible text not only establishes professionalism but also avoids inhibiting your post's visibility and engagement on the platform.

### Craft a compelling Opening Line:

Concentrate on composing a striking opening sentence, recognizing its critical role in capturing attention.

Engage your audience with an enticing, succinct, and relevant opener, employing compelling language, questions, or topical hashtags.

Significant effort should be dedicated here as an arresting start dramatically boosts the chances of your tweet being noticed and further shared.

**Be a reply guy:** Engage Intelligently as an Active Reply Contributor: but make sure your reply is long and valuable. Because only replay with values tend to be prioritized.

So actively and strategically engage in conversations on X. never be spammy.

Develop an 'X List' of vital accounts within your niche and dedicate at least 15 minutes a day to thoughtfully respond to their tweets.

Ensure your replies add substantial value to the discourse, subsequently presenting your account as an insightful and beneficial contributor to the community.

### Uphold a Consistent Posting Schedule:

Cultivate and maintain an unswerving posting pattern on X.

To avoid any adverse impacts on your algorithmic positioning due to irregular posting, employ scheduling tools like Hootsuite or Buffer to orchestrate your posts in advance.

Keeping your account active and engaged, even during periods of personal unavailability, is essential for preserving and enhancing your digital presence.

### Stay in Your Niche:

Ensure all content aligns succinctly with your chosen niche to exploit algorithmic favor and nurture audience engagement.

X's algorithm categorizes accounts into clusters based on the consistency of their content topic.

Abiding by your niche and producing related content will enhance your visibility within your network.

And there are other hundreds of niche based clusters based on hundreds X user interests.

Diverging from your established content themes may result in reduced reach and engagement.

Employ analytics tools to discern which themes within your niche are most engaging and construct a content calendar leveraging these insights to sustain thematic consistency and relevance.

### Utilize your X-Premium Subscription

Consider subscribing to X Blue to potentially augment the reach of your tweets, particularly within your network or niche, sometimes offering a substantial 2-4x boost in visibility.

Continuously scrutinize the performance metrics of your tweets to evaluate the tangible impact and ROI of utilizing X Premium subscription on your outreach and engagement.

# STRATEGIES TO MAXIMIZE YOUR X REVENUE

Thriving on X is not solely about amassing a significant follower count; it's about strategically channeling this audience to generate revenue.

The platform offers various features to monetize your content, services, or
products. Utilizing them proficiently can significantly boost your earnings.

Let us see some proven strategies to make a living on X.

### Optimized Linking:

Website and Linktree Integration: Your X account bio is the gateway to further engagement.

Include a link to your website or a Linktree page encompassing links to all products, services, affiliate partnerships, and other platforms you're active on.

This centralized link hub enhances the visitor's journey, directing them to diverse revenue streams.

### Creator X Subscription Model

Enabling Creator Subscription Button: If you offer services or products on a recurring basis, activate the Creator Subscription button.

This feature facilitates a steady income flow from dedicated followers, ensuring they never miss your latest offerings.

### Strategic Post Pinning

Effective Use of the Pinned Feature: Pinned posts are the first content pieces visitors see.

Craft a captivating ad copy for your prime services or products with a cl ear call to action or purchase link.

By pinning this post, you ensure it gain maximum visibility, acting as a perennial advertisement on your profile.

## Profile Aesthetics:

Leveraging Cover Photo: Your profile's cover photo is a billboard waitin g to be utilized.

Design a cover photo that succinctly showcases what your do or your
offerings, encapsulating everything you sell or provide. This visual cu e can intrigue visitors to explore further.

## Enroll on X Ad Revenue share program.

Enrolling in the X Ad Revenue Share Program can unlock an additional revenue avenue. By sharing ad revenues, X offers a lucrative way to monetize your content further.

## End of Post Call to Actions (CTAs)

At the end of your post, consider congratulating readers for reaching the conclusion. Incorporate a CTA encouraging them to follow you for more insights.

Also, remind them of the products or services available on your profile,
which may entice them to make a purchase or visit your profile.

This leads to more profile visits signal to X's algorithm a higher level of engagement, and increased revenue.

Here is the example.

"Congrats on reaching the end! Follow me for more and check my products on my profile."

**Used promoted tweet opportunity regularly.**

Utilize promoted tweets/Posts and ads for all your services and products. Nowadays, AI tools can create compelling ad copy that sells, so take advantage of this to increase your profit.

### Embrace New Revenue Opportunities:

Seize any Emerging money-making Features: X is continually evolving, with new money-making features being rolled out periodically.

Make it a goal to stay abreast of these updates and join any new revenue- generating program as soon as it's available.

Engaging early with new features not only provides additional revenue streams but can also position you as a forward-thinking creator within the community.

This proactive approach can lead to increased visibility and further monetization opportunities as you adapt swiftly to the platform's evolving landscape.

**Networking and Collaboration**: Engage with other successful creators on X to gain insights into emerging revenue opportunities.

Collaboration can also lead to cross-promotional activities, expanding your audience and potential customer base.

By fostering a supportive network, you can learn and grow together, maximizing revenue generation on X.

**Continuous Learning**: Participate in webinars, workshops, and online courses that focus on monetization strategies on X.

Acquiring new knowledge and skills will enable you to leverage new revenue-generating features effectively, ensuring you are always                            at                            the forefront of monetization opportunities on the platform.

Adapting to new revenue channels and leveraging collaborative netw orks are vital strategies for maximizing earnings on X.

By staying informed, engaging with the community, and continually learni ng, you can significantly enhance your revenue generation potential on the platform.

Congrats on reaching the end! check my other books below

# ABOUT THE AUTHOR

## Ibrahim John

Ibrahim John is a seasoned entrepreneur and business consultant, with a passion for helping others achieve financial stability and success.

Ibrahim founded his first company while still in college in 2013, and since then has gone on to establish a total of three successful companies: Agrasa Agriculture Limited, Kingbest Company Limited, and Nzunda Technologies Limited.

His experience in both the IT and business sectors has given him a unique skill set that he uses to help others register their companies, marketing, Brandind and Social Media Management

# BOOKS BY THIS AUTHOR

## The Art Of Solving A Lack Of Money Problem And Escaping The Rat Race

This book is a Complete Guide for Overcoming Financial Struggles and Achieving Wealth. It offers a step-by-step proven "Effectuation approach" to overcome financial struggles and to build wealth, so you can achieve financial stability and live the life you deserve

And it gives you strategies to change any level of financial status quo you have right now. Whether you are low-income, middle- high-income class, or just an entrepreneur,

With clear, concise guidance, this book will help you develop the money mindset and skills you need to succeed.

## The Art Of Asking ChatGPT For High-Quality Answers

This book is GPT-4 & ChatGPT Plugins updated. A comprehensive guide to understanding and utilizing various prompt techniques to generate high-quality answers from ChatGPT. and How To Avoid & Bypass all A.I Content Detectors

1: This book is on point, I have used simple language with on-point practical explanations, together with examples and prompt formulas on every prompt technique.We don't want to waste your time with our stories. just on point. no stories.

NB: we have fixed editing errors and previous formatting issues

2: My aim is for you to understand the underlying principles, which will enable you to use any version of ChatGPT in an advanced way without memorizing any formulas. This eliminates the need for having thousands of formulas, which, in fact, are based on the same principles.

3: Examples provided in this book are designed to help you comprehend these principles. After finishing this book, you won't need any lists, such as 1,000 prompt formulas

NB: We appreciate that you've chosen to purchase this book with the intention of expanding your knowledge and exploring new concepts. We kindly ask that you approach the content with an open mind, focusing on the learning opportunities it provides, RATHER THAN solely seeking confirmation of the information you already possess.

We explore how different prompt engineering techniques can be used to achieve other goals. ChatGPT is a state-of-the-art language model that is capable of generating human-like text. However, it is vital to understand the right way to ask ChatGPT in order to get the high-quality outputs we desire.

4. With this book, you'll learn how to use prompt engineering techniques to control the output of ChatGPT and generate text tailored to your specific needs.

5. Throughout this book, we also provide examples of how to combine different prompt techniques to achieve more specific outcomes.

I hope you will find this book as informative and enjoyable as I enjoyed writing it.

## The Manipulated Buyer: Discover How Most Marketers & Gurus Trick You Into Buying What They Sell

In this book, I share my experiences and research into the marketing world. I show you how to spot the red flags and teach you how to make better purchasing decisions

So, in this 2in1 book you will learn the following;

1. How to recognize manipulation tactics if they exist in any advertisement you interact with. In order not to fall into the traps of "manipulative marketers"

2. Advanced marketing tricks to prepare an ad in quality without manipulating customers,

3. The best ways to make a customer buy your product or service without coercion

4. After reading this book, you will become an "EXPERT" in marketing and Copywriting. Because your eyes will be opened; you will start to see openly everything that goes on in the world of marketing and copywriting.